ROBERT LOUIS STEVENSON

BY

G. K. CHESTERTON

Author of
"Heretics," "Orthodoxy,"
"The Everlasting Man," Etc.

NEW YORK
DODD, MEAD & COMPANY
1928

CONTENTS

11211

"THE MYTH OF STEVENSON"

CHAPTER I

"THE MYTH OF STEVENSON"

In this brief study of Stevenson I propose to follow a somewhat unusual course; or to sketch what may be considered a rather eccentric outline. It can only be justified in practice; and I have a healthy fear that my practice will not justify it. Nevertheless, I have not adopted it without considerable thought, and even doubt, about the best way of dealing with a real and practical problem. So before it collapses completely in practice, I will give myself the triumph and the joy of justifying it in principle.

The difficulty arises thus. In the great days of Stevenson critics had begun to be ashamed of being critics, and of giving to their ancient function the name of criticism. It was the fashion to publish a book that was a bundle of reviews and to call it "Appreciations." But the world advances; and if that sort of book is published now, it might well bear the general title of "Depreciations." Stevenson has suffered more than most from this new fashion of minimising and finding fault; and some energetic and successful writers have thrown themselves into the business almost with the eagerness of stock-brokers, bent on making a slump instead of a boom in Stevenson Stock. It may be questioned whether we need welcome the bear any more than the bull in the china-shop of elegant English letters. Others seem to make quite a hobby of proving a particular writer to be overrated. They write long and laborious articles, full of biographical detail and bitter commentary, in order to show that the subject is unworthy of attention; and write pages upon Stevenson to prove that he is not worth writing about. Neither their motives nor their methods are very clear or satisfactory. If it be true that all swans are geese to the discriminating eye of the scientific ornithologist, it hardly suffices to explain so long or so fatiguing a wild-goose chase.

But it is true that, in a sense more general than that of these rather irritable individuals, such a reaction does exist. And it is a reaction against Stevenson, or at least against Stevensonians. Perhaps it would be most correct to call it a reaction against Stevensoniana. And let me say at this early stage that I heartily agree that there has been far too much Stevensoniana. In one sense, indeed, everything about anybody so interesting as Stevenson is interesting.

In one sense, everything about everybody is interesting. But not everybody can interest everybody else: and it is well to know an author is loved, but not to publish all the love-letters. Sometimes we only had to endure that most awful and appalling tragedy: a truth told once too often. Sometimes we heard Stevensonian sentiments repeated in violation of all Stevensonian rules. For of all things he hated dilution: and loved to take language neat, like a liqueur. In short, it was overdone; it was too noisy and yet all on one note; above all, it was too incessant and too prolonged. As I say, there were a variety of causes, which it would be unnecessary and sometimes unamiable to discuss. There was perhaps something in it of the very virtue of Stevenson; he was tolerant of many societies and interested in many men; and there was nothing to ward off the direst results of the men being interested in him. Especially after he was dead, one person after another turned up and wrote a book about meeting Stevenson on a steamboat or in a restaurant; and it is not surprising that such book-makers began to look as vulgar as bookies. There was perhaps something in it of the old joke of Johnson: that the Scots are in a conspiracy to praise each other. It was often because the Scots are secret sentimentalists and cannot always keep the secret. Their interest in a story so brilliant and in some ways so pathetic was perfectly natural and human; but for all that, their interest was overdone. It was sometimes, I regret to say, because the interest might fairly be called a vested interest. Anyhow, any number of things happened to combine to vulgarise the thing; but vulgarising a thing does not really make it vulgar.

Now Stevenson's life was really what we call picturesque; partly because he saw everything in pictures; and partly because a chapter of accidents did really attach him to very picturesque places. He was born on the high terraces of the noblest of northern cities: in the family mansion in Edinburgh in 1850; he was the son of a house of highly respected architects of lighthouses; and nothing could be more really romantic than such a legend of men laboriously lifting the star-crowned towers of the sea. He failed to follow the family tradition, however, for various reasons; he was blighted with ill-health and a taste for art; the latter sent him to pick up picturesque tricks and poses in the art colony of Barbizon; the former very soon sent him southward into warmer and warmer climates; and it so happens as he himself remarked, that the countries to which we are sent when health deserts us have a magical and rather mocking beauty. At one time he had paid a sort of vagabond visit to America, crossing the ugly plains that lead to the abrupt beauty of California, that promised land. He described it in the studies called *Across the Plain:* a work vaguely unsatisfying both to writer and reader. I think it records the subconscious blank and sense of bewilderment felt by every true European on first seeing the very light and landscape of America. The shock of negation was in his case truly unnatural. He almost wrote a dull book. But there is another reason for noting this exception here.

This book makes no pretence of being even an outline of the life of Stevenson. In his particular case I deliberately omit such an outline, because I find that it has cut across and confused the very sharp and lucid outline of his art. But indeed in any case it would be very difficult to tell the tale with truth without telling it in detail, and in rather bewildering detail. The first thing that strikes us, on a rapid survey of his life and letters, is his innumerable changes of domicile, especially in his early days. If his friends followed the example he professes to set, in the matter of Mr. Michael Finsbury, and refused to learn more than one address for one friend, he must have left his correspondence very far behind indeed. His wanderings in Western Europe would appear on the map as much wilder as well as wider than the "probable course of David Balfour's wanderings" in Western Scotland. If we started out to tell his story thus, we should have to note how he went first to Mentone and then back again to Edinburgh and then to Fontaine-bleau and then to the Highlands and then to Fontainebleau again and then to Davos in the mountains, and so on; a zigzag pilgrimage impossible to compress except in a larger biography. But all or most of it is covered by one generalisation. This navigation chart was really a hospital chart. Its jagged mountains represented temperatures; or at least climates. The whole story of Stevenson is conditioned by a certain complexity, which a tenderness for the English language will restrain us from calling a complex. It was a sort of paradox, by which he was at once more and less protected than other men; like somebody travelling the wildest roads of the world in a covered waggon. He went where he did partly because he was an adventurer and partly because he was an invalid. By that sort of limping agility, he may be said to have seen at once too little and too much. He was perhaps a natural traveller; but he was not a normal traveller. Nobody ever did treat him as quite normal; which is the truth hidden in the falsehood of those who sneer at his childishness as that of a spoilt child. He was courageous; and yet he had to be shielded against two things at once, his weakness and his courage. But his picture of himself as a vagabond with blue fingers on the winter road is avowedly an ideal picture; it was exactly that sort of freedom that he could never have. He could only be carried from sight to sight; or even from adventure to adventure. Indeed there is here a curious aptness in the quaint simplicity of his childish rhyme that ran, "My bed is like a little boat." Through all his varied experiences his bed was a boat and his boat was a bed. Panoramas of tropic palm and Californian orange-grove passed over that moving couch like the long nightmare of the nursery walls. But his real courage was not so much turned outwards to the drama of the boat as inwards to the drama of the bed. Nobody knew better than he did that nothing is more terrible than a bed; since it is always waiting to be a deathbed.

Broadly speaking, therefore, his biography would consist of journeys hither and thither, with a donkey in the Cevennes, with a baronet on the French canals; on a sledge in Switzerland or in a bathchair at Bournemouth. But they were all, in one way or another, related to the problem of his health as well as to the cheerfulness of his curiosity. Now of all human things the search for health is the most unhealthy. And it is truly a great glory to Stevenson that he, almost alone among men, could go on pursuing his bodily health without once losing his mental health. As soon as he came to any place, he lost no time in finding a new and better reason for having come there. It might be a child or a sonnet, a flirtation or the plan of a story; but he made that the real reason; and not the unhealthy reason of health. Nevertheless, there generally had been, somewhere in the background, some suggestion of the reason of health; as there was in that last great journey to his final home in the South Seas.

The one real break, I suspect, in this curious double process of protection and risk, was his breakaway to America, which arose partly at least in connection with the matter of his marriage. It seemed to his friends and family, not so much like the conduct of an invalid who had done a bolt from the hospital, as the conduct of a lunatic unaccountably loose from the asylum. In truth, the voyage struck them as less mad than the marriage. As this is not a biographical study, I need not go deeply into the delicate disputes about that business; but it was admittedly at least unconventional. All that matters to the argument here is that, while there was much in it that was even noble, it was not normal. It was not love as it should come to youth: it is no disrespect to either to say that in both, psychologically speaking, there was an element of patching up as well as of binding together. Stevenson had met, first in Paris and later in America, an American lady married to a seemingly somewhat unsatisfactory American gentleman, against whom she took proceedings for divorce. Stevenson at the same time precipitately crossed the seas and in some sense pursued her to California; I suppose with some vague idea of being in at the death; and indeed he was very nearly in at his own. The escapade brought on him one of the worst and sharpest of his attacks of illness; the lady, being on the spot, naturally threw herself into nursing him; and as soon as he could stand on two rickety legs they were married. It caused consternation to his family, who were however really reconciled afterwards, it would seem, by the personal magnetism of his foreign and almost exotic bride. Certainly in her society his literary work went with a renewed swing and even regularity; and the rest of his story is practically the story of his important works; varied by his, if possible, still more important friendships. There was illness, in which, it should be said, it was often a case of two invalids nursing each other. Then came the decision to fall back on the secure climate of the Pacific Islands; which led to his taking up his last station at Vailima on the island of Samoa: in a coloured archipelago which our cheerful forefathers might have described as the Cannibal Islands, but which Stevenson was more disposed to describe as the Islands of the Blest. There he lived as happily as can an exile who loves his country and his friends, free at least of all the daily dangers of his lung trouble; and there he died, very suddenly, at the age of forty-four, the beloved patriarch of a little white and brown community, to whom he was known as Tusitala or the Teller of Tales.

That is the main outline of the actual biography of Robert Louis Stevenson; and from the time when he clambered as a boy among the crags and castellations of the Painted Hill, looking across the islets of the Forth, to the time when tall brown barbarians, crowned with red flowers, bore him on their spears to the peak of their sacred mountain, the spirit of this artist had been permitted to inhabit, and as it were to haunt, the beautiful places of the earth. To the last he had tasted that beauty with a burning sensibility; and it is no joke, in his case, to say that he would have enjoyed coming to his own funeral.

Of course, even this generalisation is too much of a simplification. He was not, as we shall later have occasion to note, unacquainted with sombre nor, alas, with sordid surroundings. Oscar Wilde said with some truth that Stevenson might have produced yet richer and more purple romances if he had always lived in Gower Street; and he was certainly one of the very few who have managed to feel fierce and adventurous at Bournemouth. But broadly speaking, it is true that the outline of his life was romantic; and was therefore perhaps too easily turned into a romance. He himself deliberately turned it into a romance; but not all those romancing were such good romancers as he. So the romance tended to turn into mere repetition and gossip; and the romantic figure faded into journalism as the figure of Robin Hood faded into endless penny dreadfuls or schoolboy serials; as the figure of Micawber was multiplied and cheapened into Ally Sloper. Then came the reaction; a reaction which I should call rather excusable than justifiable. But that reaction is the problem in any popular treatment of him to-day.

Now if I were to follow here the natural course of such a volume as this, I should have to begin by telling slowly and systematically the tale that I have just told rapidly and briefly. I should have to give a chapter to his childhood, to his favourite aunt and his yet more beloved nurse, and to all the things much more clearly recorded in *A Child's Garden of Verses*. I should have to give a chapter to his youth, his differences with his father, his struggles with his malady, his greater struggles about his marriage; working up slowly through the whole length of the book to the familiar picture of so many magazines and memoirs; the slender semi-tropical Tusitala with his long brown hair and long olive face and long strange slits of eyes, sitting clad in white or crowned with garlands and telling tales to all the tribes of men. Now the misfortune of all this would be that it would amount to saying, through a slow series of chapters, that there is nothing more to be said about Stevenson except what has been said a thousand times. It would be to suggest that Stevenson's serious fame does still really depend on this string of picturesque accidents; and that there is really nothing to be told of him, except that he wore long hair in the Savile Club or light clothes in the Samoan mountains. His life really was romantic; but to repeat that romance is like reprinting the *Scarlet Pimpernel* or offering the world an entirely new portrait of Rudolph Valentino. It is against this repetition that the reaction has set in; perhaps wrongly but certainly strongly. And to spin it out through the whole of this book would be to give the impression (which I should mildly resent) that this book is only the thousandth unnecessary volume of Stevensoniana. However I told his story in detail, though it were with all the sympathy I feel, I could not avoid that suggestion of a sort of jaded journalism. Stevenson's picturesque attitude and career are rather in his way at this moment; not for me, because I like the picturesque, but for this new pose which may be called the pose of the prosaic. To these unfortunate realists, to say that there were all these romantic things about him is only another way of saying that there was nothing in him. And there was a very great deal in him. I am driven to adopt some other method of bringing it out.

When I come to describing it, I find it is perhaps even more difficult to describe it than to do it. But something of this sort is what I propose to do. Loudon Dodd, in whom there is much of Louis Stevenson, says very truly in *The Wrecker*, that for the artist the external result is always a fizzle: his eyes are turned inward: "he lives for a state of mind." I mean to attempt the conjectural description of certain states of mind, with the books that were the "external expression" of them. If for the artist his art is a fizzle, his life is often far more of a fizzle: it is even far more of a fiction. It is the one of his works in which he tells least of the truth. Stevenson's was more real than most, because more romantic than most. But I prefer the romances, which were still more real. I mean that I think the wanderings of Balfour more Stevensonian than the wanderings of Stevenson: that the duel of Jekyll and Hyde is more illuminating than the quarrel of Stevenson and Henley: and that the true private life is to be sought not in Samoa but in Treasure Island; for where the treasure is, there is the heart also.

In short, I propose to review his books with illustrations from his life; rather than to write his life with illustrations from his books. And I do it deliberately, not because his life was not as interesting as any book; but because the habit of talking too much about his life has already actually led to thinking far too little of his literature. His ideas are being underrated, precisely because they are not being studied separately and seriously as ideas. His art is being underrated, precisely because he is not accorded even the fair advantages of Art for Art's Sake. There is indeed a queer irony about the fate of the men of that age, who delighted in that axiom. They claimed judgement as artists, not men; and they are really remembered as men much more than they are remembered as artists. More men know the Whistlerian anecdotes than the Whistlerian etchings; and poor Wilde will live in history as immoral rather than unmoral. But there is a real reason for studying intrinsic intellectual values in the case of Stevenson; and it need not be said that exactly where the modern maxim would be useful, it is never used. The new criticism of Stevenson is still a criticism of Stevenson rather than of Stevenson's work; it is always a personal criticism, and often, I think, rather a spiteful criticism. It is simply nonsense, for instance, for a distinguished living novelist to suggest that Stevenson's correspondence is a thin stream of selfish soliloquy devoid of feeling for anybody but himself. It teems with lively expressions of longing for particular people and places; it breaks out everywhere with delight into that broad Scots idiom which, as Stevenson truly said elsewhere, gives a special freedom to all the terms of affection. Stevenson might be lying, of course, though I know not why a busy author should lie at such length for nothing. But I cannot see how any man could say any more to suggest his dependence on the society of friends. These are positive facts of personality that can never be proved or disproved. I never knew Stevenson; but I knew very many of his favourite friends and correspondents. I knew Henry James and William Archer; I have still the honour of knowing Sir James Barrie and Sir Edmund Gosse. And anybody who knows them, even most slightly and superficially, must know they are not the men to be in confidential correspondence for years with a silly, greedy and exacting egoist without seeing through him; or to be bombarded with boring autobiographies without being bored. But it seems rather a pity that such critics should still be called upon to hunt up Stevenson's letter-bag, when they might well think it time to form some conclusions about Stevenson's place in letters. Anyhow, I propose on the present occasion to be so perverse as to interest myself in literature when dealing with a literary man; and to be especially interested not only in the literature left by the man but in the philosophy inhering in the literature. And I am especially interested in a certain story, which was indeed the story of his life, but not exactly the story in his biography. It was an internal and spiritual story; and the stages of it are to be found rather in his stories than in his external acts. It is told much better in the difference between *Treasure Island* and *The Story of a Lie*, or in the difference between *A Child's Garden of Verses* and *Markheim* or *Olalla*, than in any detailed account of his wrangles with his father or the fragmentary love-affairs of his youth. For it seems to me that there is a moral to the art of Stevenson (if the shades of Wilde and Whistler will endure the challenge), and that it is one with a real bearing on the future of European culture and the hope that is to guide our children. Whether I shall be able to draw out this moral and make it sufficiently large and clear, I know as little as the reader does.

Nevertheless, at this stage of the attempt I will say one thing. I have, in a sense, a sort of theory about Stevenson; a view of him which, right or wrong, concerns his life and work as a whole. But it is perhaps less exclusively personal than much of the interest that has been naturally taken in his personality. It is certainly the very contrary of the attacks which have commonly, and especially recently, been made on that personality. Thus the critics are fond of suggesting that he was nothing if not self-conscious; that the whole of his significance came from self-consciousness. I believe that the one really great and important work which he did for the world was done quite unconsciously. Many have blamed him for posing; some have blamed him for preaching. The matter which mainly interests me is not merely his pose, if it was a pose, but the large landscape or background against which he was posing; which he himself only partly realised, but which goes to make up a rather important historical picture. And though it is true that he sometimes preached, and preached very well, I am by no means certain that the thing which he preached was the same as the thing which he taught. Or, to put it another way, the thing which he could teach was not quite so large as the thing which we can learn. Or again, many of them declare that he was only a nine days' wonder, a passing figure that happened to catch the eye and even affect the fashion; and that with that fashion he will be forgotten. I believe that the lesson of his life will only be seen after time has revealed the full meaning of all our present tendencies; I believe it will be seen from afar off like a vast plan or maze traced out on a hillside; perhaps traced by one who did not even see the plan while he was making the tracks. I believe that his travels and doublings and returns reveal an idea, and even a doctrine. Yet it was perhaps a doctrine in which he did not believe, or at any rate did not believe that he believed. In other words, I think his significance will stand out more strongly in relation to larger problems which are beginning to press once more upon the mind of man; but of which many men are still largely unaware in our time, and were almost entirely unaware in his. But any contribution to the solution of those problems will be remembered; and he made a very great contribution, probably greater than he knew. Lastly, these same critics do not hesitate, in many cases, to accuse him flatly of being insincere. I should say that nobody, so openly fond of play-acting as he was, could possibly be insincere. But it is more to my purpose now to say that his relation to the huge half-truth that he carried was in its very simplicity a mark of truthfulness. For he had the splendid and ringing sincerity to testify, in a voice like a trumpet, to a truth that he did not understand.

IN THE COUNTRY OF SKELT

CHAPTER II

IN THE COUNTRY OF SKELT

EVERY now and then the eye is riveted, in reading current criticism, by some statement so astonishingly untrue, or even contrary to the fact, that it seems as if a man walking down the street were suddenly standing on his head. It is all the more noticeable when the critic really has a strong head to stand on. One of the ablest of the younger critics, whose studies in other subjects I have warmly admired, wrote in our invaluable *London Mercury* a study of Stevenson; or what purported to be a study of Stevenson. And the chief thing he said, indeed almost the only thing he said, was that the thought of Stevenson instantly throws us back to the greater example of Edgar Allan Poe; that both were pallid and graceful figures "making wax flowers," as somebody said; and of course the earlier and greater had the advantage of the later and the less. In fact, the critic treated Stevenson as the shadow of Poe; which may not unfairly be called the shadow of a shade. He almost hinted that, for those who had read Poe, it was hardly worth while to read Stevenson. And indeed I could almost suspect he had taken his own advice; and never read a line of Stevenson in his life.

If a man were to say that Maeterlinck derives so directly from Dickens that it is difficult to draw the line between them, I should be momentarily at a loss to catch his meaning. If he were to say that Walt Whitman was so close a copyist of Pope that it is hardly worth while to read the copy, I should not at once seize the clue. But I should think these comparisons rather more close, if anything, than the comparison between Stevenson and Poe. Dickens did not confine himself to comic subjects so much as Poe did to tragic ones; and an Essay on Optimism might couple the names of Pope and Whitman. It might also include the name of Stevenson; but it would hardly beam and sparkle with the name of Poe. The contrast, however, is much deeper than labels or the commonplaces of controversy. It is much deeper than formal divisions between what is funny and what is serious. It is concerned with something which it is now fashionable in drawing-rooms to call psychological; but which those who would as soon talk Latin as Greek still prefer to call spiritual. It is not necessarily what the newspapers would call moral; but that is only because it is more moral than most modern morality.

When Stevenson was known as Stennis, by Parisian art students struggling with his name, it was the hour of Art for Art's Sake. Painting was to be impersonal, though painters (like Whistler) were sometimes perhaps a little personal. But they all insisted that every picture is as impersonal as a pattern. They ought to have insisted that every pattern is as personal as a picture. Whether or no we see faces in the carpet, we ought to see a mind in the carpet; and in fact there is a mind in every scheme of ornament. There is as emphatically a morality expressed in Babylonian architecture or Baroque architecture as if it were plastered all over with Biblical texts. Now in the same manner there is at the back of every artist's mind something like a pattern or a type of architecture. The original quality in any man of imagination is imagery. It is a thing like the landscapes of his dreams; the sort of world he would wish to make or in which he would wish to wander; the strange flora and fauna of his own secret planet; the *sort* of thing that he likes to think about. This general atmosphere, and pattern or structure of growth, governs all his creations however varied; and because

[27]

he can in this sense create a world, he is in this sense
a creator; the image of God. Now everybody knows
what was in this sense the atmosphere and architecture of Poe. Dark wine, dying lamps, drugging
odours, a sense of being stifled in curtains of black
velvet, a substance which is at once utterly black
and unfathomably soft, all carried with them a sense
of indefinite and infinite decay. The word infinite is
not itself used indefinitely. The point of Poe is that
we feel that *everything* is decaying, including ourselves; faces are already growing featureless like those
of lepers; roof-trees are rotting from root to roof;
one great grey fungus as vast as a forest is sucking
up life rather than giving it forth; mirrored in stag-
nant pools like lakes of poison which yet fade without line or frontier into the swamp. The stars are not
clean in his sight; but are rather more worlds made
for worms. And this corruption is increased, by an
intense imaginative genius, with the addition of a
satin surface of luxury and even a terrible sort of
comfort. "Purple cushions that the lamplight gloated
o'er" is in the spirit of his brother Baudelaire who
wrote of *divans profonds commes les tombeaux*. This
dark luxury has something almost liquid about it. Its
laxity seems to be betraying more vividly how all
these things are being sucked away from us, down

a slow whirlpool more like a moving swamp. That is the atmosphere of Edgar Allan Poe; a sort of rich rottenness of decomposition, with something thick and narcotic in the very air. It is idle to describe what so darkly and magnificently describes itself. But perhaps the shortest and best way of describing that artistic talent is to say that Stevenson's is exactly the opposite.

The first fact about the imagery of Stevenson is that all his images stand out in very sharp outline; and are, as it were, all edges. It is something in him that afterwards attracted him to the abrupt and angular black and white of woodcuts. It is to be seen from the first, in the way in which his eighteenth-century figures stand up against the skyline, with their cutlasses and cocked hats. The very words carry the sound and the significance. It is as if they were cut out with cutlasses; as was that unforgettable chip or wedge that was hacked by the blade of Billy Bones out of the wooden sign of the "Admiral Benbow." That sharp indentation of the wooden square remains as a sort of symbolic shape expressing Stevenson's type of literary attack; and if all the colours should fade from me and the scene of all that romance grow dark, I think that black wooden sign with a piece bitten out of it would be the last shape that I should see. It is no mere pun to say that it is the best of his woodcuts. Normally, anyhow, the scene is the very reverse of dark, and certainly the very reverse of indefinite. Just as all the form can best be described as clean-cut, so all the colour is conspicuously clear and bright. That is why such figures are so often seen standing against the sea. Everybody who has been at the seaside has noted how sharp and highly coloured, like painted caricatures, appear even the most ordinary figures as they pass in profile to and fro against the blue dado of the sea. There is something also of that hard light that falls full and pale upon ships and open shores; and even more, it need not be said, of a certain salt and acrid clearness in the air. But it is notably the case in the outlines of these maritime figures. They are all edges and they stand by the sea, that is the edge of the world.

This is but a rough experimental method; but it will be found useful to make the experiment, of calling up all the Stevensonian scenes that recur most readily to the memory; and noting this bright hard quality in shape and hue. It will make it seem all the stranger that any ornithologist could have confused the raven of Poe with the parrot of Long John Silver. The parrot was scarce more reputable; but he was a bird from the lands of bright plumage and blue skies, where the other bird was a mere shadow making darkness more dark. It is even worth noting that when the more modern pirates of *The Wrecker* carried away with them a caged bird, it had to be a canary. It is specially observed when Stevenson is dealing with things which many of his contemporaries made merely shadowy or unfathomably mysterious; such as the Highland hills and all the lost kingdoms of the Gael. His Highland tales have everything Scotch except Scotch mist. At that time, and even before, writers of the school of Fiona Macleod were already treating such peoples entirely as the Children of the Mist. But there is very little mist on the mountains of Stevenson. There is no Celtic twilight about his Celts. Alan Breck Stewart had no yearning for any delicate vapour to veil his bright silver buttons or his bright blue French coat. There was hardly a cloud in the sky upon that day of doom, when Glenure dropped dead in the sunshine; and he did not have red hair for nothing. Stevenson is even moved to mention that the servant behind him was laden with lemons; because lemons are bright yellow. This sort of making of a picture may not be conscious, but it is none the less characteristic. Of course I do not mean literally that all the scenes in any novel could have the same scheme of colour, or occur at the same time of day. There are exceptions to the rule; but even these will generally be found to be exceptions that prove the rule. A time of *A Lodging for the Night* is not unnaturally at night; but even in that nightmare of winter in mediæval Paris the mind's eye is really filled rather with the whiteness of snow than the blackness of darkness. It is against the snow that we see the flaming mediæval figures; and especially that memorable figure who (like Campbell of Glenure) had no right to have red hair when he was dead. The hair is like a scarlet splash of blood crying for vengeance; but I doubt whether the doomed gentleman in Poe's poetry would have been allowed to have red hair even when he was alive. In the same way, it would be easy to answer in detail, by finding some description of night in the works of Stevenson; but it would never be the night that broods eternally on the works of Poe. It might be said, for instance, that there are few more vivid or typical scenes in the Stevensonian tales than that of the duel at midnight in *The Master of Ballantrae.* But there again the exception proves the rule; the description insists not on the darkness of night but on the hardness of winter, the "windless stricture of the frost"; the candles that stand as straight as the swords; the candle-flames that seem almost as cold as the stars. I have spoken of the double meaning of a woodcut; this was surely, in the same double sense, a steel engraving. A steely cold stiffens and steadies that tingling play of steel; and that not only materially but morally. The House of Durrisdeer does not fall after the fashion of The House of Ussher. There is in that murderous scene I know not what that is clean and salt and sane; and, in spite of all, the white frost gives to the candles a sort of cold purification as of candlemas. But the point is, at the moment, that when we say this deed was done at night, we do not mean that it was done in the dark. There is a sense of exactitude and emphatic detail that belongs entirely to the day. Here indeed the two authors so strangely compared might almost have conspired in advance against the critic who compared them: as when Poe's ideal detective prefers to think in the dark, and therefore puts up the shutters even during the day. Dupin brings the outer darkness into the parlour, while Durie carries the candle-light into the forest.

These images are not fancies or accidents: their spirit runs through the whole scene. The same incident, for instance, shows all the author's love of sharp edges and cutting or piercing action. It is supremely typical that he made Mrs. Durie thrust the sword up to the hilt into the frozen ground. It is true that afterwards (perhaps under the sad eye of Mr. Archer and the sensitive realists) he consented to withdraw this as "an exaggeration to stagger Hugo." But it is much more significant that it did not originally stagger Stevenson. It was the very vital gesture of all his works that that sharp blade should cleave that stiff clay. It was true in many other senses, touching mortal clay and the sword of the spirit. But I am speaking now of the gesture of the craftsman, like that of a man cutting wood. This man had an appetite for cutting it clean. He never committed a murder without making a clean job of it.

Whence did that spirit come; and how did the story of it begin? That is the right and real way of beginning the story of Stevenson. If I say that it began with cutting figures out of cardboard, it might sound like a parody of the pedantic fancies about juvenile psychology and early education. But perhaps it will be better even to run the horrid risk of being mistaken for a modern educationist, rather than to repeat the too familiar phrases by which the admirer of Stevenson has got himself described as a sentimentalist. Too much has been talked in this connection about the Soul of the Child or the Peter Pan of

Samoa; not because it is untrue, but because it is a
mistake to tell a truth too often, so that it loses its
freshness; especially when it is the truth about how
to remain fresh. Many are perhaps rather tired of
hearing about it; though they would never be tired
of having it. I have therefore deliberately approached
the matter by another road; and even by a road running backwards. Instead of talking first about Cummy
and the nursery anecdotes of Master Louis (at the
risk of making a really graceful figure grow ridicu-
lous by mere repetition, in the eyes of multitudes of
greatly inferior people) I have tried to take the stock
and normal of his work first, and then note that it
really does date in a special sense from his childhood;
and that it is not sentimental and not senseless and
not irrelevant to say so.

If therefore we ask, "Where does the story of Stevenson really start; where does his special style or
spirit begin and where do they come from; how did
he get, or begin to get, the thing that made him different from the man next-door?" I have no doubt
about the answer. He got them from the mysterious
Mr. Skelt of the Juvenile Drama, otherwise the toy
theatre, which of all toys has most of the effect of
magic on the mind. Or rather, of course, he got it from
the way in which his own individual temper and tal-

ent grasped the nature of the game. He has written it all in an excellent essay and at least in one very real sentence of autobiography. "What is the world, what is man and life but what my Skelt has made them?" The psychological interest is rather more special than is conveyed by the common generalisation about the imagination of infancy. It is not merely a question of children's toys; it is a question of a particular kind of toy, as of a particular kind of talent. It was not quite the same thing, for instance, to buy toy theatres in Edinburgh as it would have been to go to real theatres in London. In that little pasteboard play there might be something of the pantomime; but there was nothing of the dissolving view. The positive outline of everything, so well sketched in his own essay, the hard favour of the heroine, the clumps of vegetation, the clouds rolled up stiff as bolsters— these things meant something to the soul of Stevenson by their very swollen solidity or angular swagger. And it is hardly an exaggeration to say that he spent his life in teaching the world what he had learnt from them. What he learnt from them was very much more than anybody else had ever learnt from them; and that is his teaching and his qualification to teach. But to the last he presented his morality in a series of Moral Emblems which had something in common with those definite outlines and defiant attitudes; and there was never any name for it but his own name of Skeltery.

It was because he loved to see on those lines, and to think in those terms, that all his instinctive images are clear and not cloudy; that he liked a gay patchwork of colour combined with a zigzag energy of action, as quick as the crooked lightning. He loved things to stand out; we might say he loved them to stick out; as does the hilt of a sabre or the feather in a cap. He loved the pattern of crossed swords; he almost loved the pattern of the gallows because it is a clear shape like the cross. And the point is that this pattern still runs through or underneath all his more mature or complex writing; and is never lost even at the moments when he is really tragic or, what is worse, realistic. Even when he mourns as a man, he still rejoices as a child. The men in divers' helmets like monsters, in the sordid misery of *The Ebb-Tide*, are still like masks of pantomime goblins against the glowing azure. And James Durie is quite as clear, we might say quite as bright, in his black coat as Alan Breck in his blue one.

Taking such a toy as a type or symbol, we may well say that Stevenson lived inside his toy theatre. It is certain that he lived in an exceptional sense inside his own home; and often, I imagine, inside his own bedroom. It is here that there appears, thus early in his life, that other element that was destined to darken it, often with something like the shadow of death. I know not how far that shadow could sometimes be traced upon the nursery wall. But it is certain that he was at least relatively a delicate or sickly child; and was therefore more thrown back upon that inner imaginative life than if he had been more robust in boyhood. The world inside that home was largely a world of his own; yes, even a world of his own imagining, a thing not so much of firelight as of pictures in the fire. The world outside his home was very different, even for those who shared his home life; and that is a contrast that I shall have occasion to emphasise, when we come to the crisis of his youth. It is enough to note here the paradox that he was to some extent protected by family life even from the heavier traditions of his family. As it did not build lighthouses in the garden pond, so it did not always bring the Kirk into the nursery. He has described how his stern Calvinistic grandfather tolerated in the nursery the wild Arabian fables that he might well have denounced in the pulpit. As even that Edinburgh house defended him from the winter winds of Edinburgh, so it protected him in some degree from the full icy blasts of Puritanism which blew so high in public life. It may have been that he was a sick child; it may have been that he was a spoilt child; but this fact that he was largely left alone with his daydreams, dwelling in that house within a house which is typified by the toy theatre, is a thing to be remembered; for it means much at a later stage.

In this matter of what has been called the Child in R. L. S., I have admitted that there has been far too much talking; but there has been far too little thinking. The thing is a reality; and it does remain as a very considerable problem for the reason, as yet quite unsolved by the modern world, even when most is said about it. We have a mass of testimony from men of every description, from Treherne to Hazlitt, or from Wordsworth to Thackeray, to the psychological fact that the child experiences joys which glow like jewels even in retrospect. None of the normal naturalistic explanations explain that natural fact; and some have suggested that it is indeed a supernatural fact. In the ordinary sense of mental growth, there is no more reason for the child being better than the man than for the tadpole being better than the frog. And the attempts to explain it by physical growth are even weaker. There is a good example of the weakness in one of the essays of Stevenson, who found himself, of course, at the particular modern moment to catch the first fashion and excitement of Darwinism. Speaking of the old Calvinist minister who confessed the gorgeous spell of the *Arabian Nights,* he suggests that in the brain of the theologian there is still the gambolling ape; the ancestor of man; "probably arboreal." It marks the security of such science, I may remark, that anthropologists are now saying that he was probably not arboreal. But anyhow, it is a little difficult to see why a man should love the complexity of labyrinthine cities, or wish to ride with the jewelled cohorts of the high princes of Arabia, merely because his relative had once been a hairy beast clambering like a bear on the top of a branching pole. It reminds one of the glorious apology which Stevenson made for having expected that a wealthy man would know a Governor of Christ's Hospital: "A man with a cold in his head does not necessarily know a rat-catcher; and the connection, as it appears to my humbled and awakened sense, is equally close."

The connection between the expanding energy of the young monkey and the secret daydreams of the young child is equally close. As a matter of fact, the time when the boy is most full of the energy of a monkey is emphatically not the time when the child is most full of the imaginative pleasures of a poet. These always come at a less vigorous period; they very often come to a less vigorous person. They especially and notably did so in the case of Stevenson; and it is absurd to explain the intensity of an infant who is an invalid by the bodily exuberance of a lad at the time when he is often rather a lout. Stevenson, with all the advantage of his disadvantages, may have lived through the period when everybody has a touch of loutishness. But that uncomfortable period of youth was not the period when the coloured pictures in his mind were most clear; they were much clearer later in the age of self-control and earlier in the age of innocence. The main point to be seized here is that they were coloured pictures of a particular kind. The colours faded, but in a certain sense the forms remained fixed; that is, that though they were slowly discoloured by the light of common day, yet when the lantern was again lit from within, the same magic-lantern slides glowed upon the blank screen. They were still pictures of pirates and red gold and bright blue sea, as they were in his childhood. And this fact is very important in the story of his mind; as we shall see when his mind reverted to them. For the time was to come when he was truly, like Jim Hawkins, to be rescued by a leering criminal with crutch and cutlass from destiny worse than death and men worse than Long John Silver—from the last phase of the enlightened nineteenth century and the leading thinkers of the age.

CHAPTER III

YOUTH AND EDINBURGH

YOUTH AND EDINBURGH

IT is the suggestion of this chapter that when Stevenson first stepped out of his early Edinburgh home, he slipped upon the step. It may have been nothing worse, to begin with, than the ordinary butter-slide of the buffoonery of youth; such buffoonery as makes up the typical Edinburgh tale called *The Misadventures of John Nicholson*. But that tale alone would suggest that there was something a little greasy or even grimy about the butter. It is an odd story for Stevenson to have written; and no Stevensonian has any particular desire to dwell on those few of his works that might almost have been written by somebody else. But it has a biographical importance that has hardly been properly estimated, even in connection with this rather overworked biography. It is a curiously unlovely and uncomfortable comedy, not even uncomfortable enough to be a tragedy. The hero is not only not heroic, but he is hardly more amusing than attractive; and the fun that is made of him is not only not genial, but is not particularly funny.

It is strange that such misadventures should come from the mind that gave us the radiant harlequinade of *The Wrong Box*. But I mention it here because it is full of a certain atmosphere, into which Stevenson was plunged too abruptly, as I believe, when he passed from boyhood into youth. It is true to call it the atmosphere, or one of the atmospheres of Edinburgh; yet it is the very reverse of so much that we rightly associate with the arid dignity of the Modern Athens. There is something very specially sordid and squalid in the glimpses of low life given in the dissipations of John Nicholson; and something of the same kind comes to us like a gust of gas from the medical students of *The Body Snatcher*. When I say that this first step of Stevenson led him rather abruptly astray, I do not mean that he did anything half so bad as multitudes of polite persons have done in the most polished centres of civilisation. But I do mean that his city was not, in that particular aspect, very polite or polished or even particularly civilised. And I notice it because it has been noticed too little; and some other things have been noticed too much.

It is an obvious truth that Stevenson was born of a Puritan tradition, in a Presbyterian country, where still rolled the echoes, at least, of the theological thunders of Knox; and where the Sabbath was sometimes

more like a day of death than a day of rest. It is
easy, only too easy, to apply this by representing
Stevenson's father as a stern old Covenanter who
frowned down the gay talents of his son; and such a
simplification stands out boldly in black and white.
But like many other black and white statements, it
is not true; it is not even fair. Old Mr. Stevenson
was a Presbyterian and presumably a Puritan, but
he was not a Pharisee; and he certainly did not need
to be a Pharisee in order to condemn some parts of
the conduct of his son. It is probably true that almost
any other son might have offended equally; but it is
also true that almost any other father would have
been equally offended. The son would have been the
last to pretend that the faults were all on one side;
the only thing that can concern posterity in the matter is certain social conditions which gave to those
faults a particular savour, which counted for something even when the faults themselves have been long
left behind. And while people have written rather too
much about the shadow of the Kirk and the restric-
tions of a Puritan society, there is something that has
not been seen about what may be called the under-
side of such a Puritan city. There is something
strangely ugly and ungracious not merely about the
virtues but about the vices, and especially the pleas-

[47]

ures, of such a place. It can be felt, as I say, in Stevenson's own stories and in many other stories about Edinburgh. Blasts of raw whisky come to us on that raw wind: there is sometimes something shrill, like the skirl of the pipes, about Scottish laughter; occasionally something very nearly insane about Scottish intoxication. I will not connect it, as did a friend of mine, with the hypothesis that the heathen Scots originally worshipped demons; but it is probably connected with the same rather savage intensity which gave them their theological thoroughness. Anyhow, it is true that in such a world even temptation itself has something terrifying as well as tempting; and yet something at the same time undignified and flat. It was this that cut across the natural poetic adventure or ambition of a young poet; and gave to the early part of his story a quality of frustration, if not of aberration.

What was the matter with Stevenson, I fancy, in so far as there was ever anything much the matter with him, was that there was too sharp a contrast between the shelter and delicate fancies of his childhood and the sort of world which met him like the wind on the front door-step. It was not merely the contrast between poetry and Puritanism; it was also the contrast between poetry and prose; and prose that was almost repulsively prosaic. He did not believe enough in Puritanism to cling to it; but he did believe very much in a potential poetry of life, and he was bewildered by its apparently impossible position in the world of real living. And his national religion, even if he had believed in his religion as ardently as he believed in his nation, would never have met that particular point at issue.

Puritanism had no idea of purity. We might almost say that there is every other virtue in Puritanism except purity; often including continence, which is quite a different thing from purity. But it has not many images of positive innocence; of the things that are at once white and solid, like the white chalk or white wood which children love. This does not detract at all from the noble Puritan qualities: the republican simplicity, the fighting spirit, the thrift, the logic, the renunciation of luxuries, the resistance to tyrants, the energy and enterprise which have helped to give the Scot his adventurous advantage all over the world. But it is none the less true that there has been in his creed, at best, negative rather than positive purity: the difference between the blank white window and the ivory tower. I know that a Victorian prejudice still regards this interpretation of history by theology as a piece of most distressing bad taste.

I also know that this taboo on the main topic of mankind is becoming an intolerable nuisance; and preventing anybody, from the Papist to the atheist, from saying what he really thinks about the most real themes in the world. And I will take the liberty of stating, in spite of the taboo, that it is really relevant here to remember this Puritan defect. It is as much a fact that the Kirk of Stevenson's country had no cult of the Holy Child, no feast of the Holy Innocents, no tradition of the Little Brothers of St. Francis, nothing that could in any way *carry on* the childish enthusiasm for simple things, and link it up with a lifelong rule of life—this is as much a fact as that the Quakers are not a good military school or the good Moslem a good wine-taster. Hence it followed that when Stevenson left his home, he shut the door on a house lined with fairy gold, but he came out on a frightful contrast; on temptations at once attractive and repulsive, and terrors that were still depressing even when they were disregarded. The boy in such surroundings is torn by something worse than the dilemma of Tannhäuser. He wonders why he is attracted by repellent things.

I will here make what is a mere guess in the dark; and in a very dark matter of the mind. But I suspect that it was originally out of this chasm of ugly division that there rose that two-headed monster, the mystery of Jekyll and Hyde. There is indeed one peculiarity about that grim grotesque which I have never seen noted anywhere; though I dare say it may have been noted more than once. It will be realised that I am not, alas, so close a student of Stevensoniana as many who seem to think much less of Stevenson. But it seems to me that the story of Jekyll and Hyde, which is presumably presented as happening in London, is all the time very unmistakably happening in Edinburgh. More than one of the characters seem to be pure Scots. Mr. Utterson, the lawyer, is a most unmistakably Scottish lawyer, strictly occupied with Scots Law. No modern English lawyer ever read a book of dry divinity in the evening merely because it was Sunday. Mr. Hyde indeed possesses the cosmopolitan charm that unites all nations; but there is something decidedly Caledonian about Dr. Jekyll; and especially something that calls up that quality in Edinburgh that led an unkind observer (probably from Glasgow) to describe it as "an east-windy, west-endy place." The particular tone about his respectability, and the horror of mixing his reputation with mortal frailty, belongs to the upper middle classes in solid Puritan communities. But what is especially to the point of the present argument, there is a sense

[51]

in which that Puritanism is expressed even more in Mr. Hyde than in Dr. Jekyll. The sense of the sudden stink of evil, the immediate invitation to step into stark filth, the abruptness of the alternative between that prim and proper pavement and that black and reeking gutter—all this, though doubtless involved in the logic of the tale, is far too frankly and familiarly offered not to have had some basis in observation and reality. It is not thus that the ordinary young pagan, of warmer climes, conceives the alternative of Christ and Aphrodite. His imagination and half his mind are involved in defending the beauty and dignity of the joy of gods and men. It is not so that Stevenson himself came to talk of such things, when he had felt the shadow of old Athens fall on the pagan side of Paris. I allow for all the necessary horror of the conception of Hyde. But this dingy quality does not belong only to the demon antics of Hyde. It is implied, somehow, in every word about the furtive and embarrassed vices of Jekyll. It is the tragedy of a Puritan town; every bit as much as that black legend which Stevenson loved, in which the walking-stick of Major Weir went walking down the street all by itself. I hope to say something in a moment about the very deep and indeed very just and wise morality that is really involved in that ugly tale. I am

only remarking here that the atmosphere and setting
of it are those of some tale of stiff hypocrisy in a
rigid sect or provincial village; it might be a tale of
the Middle West savagely dissected in the Spoon
River Anthology. But the point about it is that the
human beauty which makes sin most dangerous
hardly appears by a hint; this Belial is never graceful
or humane; and in this there seems to me to be something suggestive of the inverted order and ugly contrast with which licence presents itself in a world
that has frowned on liberty. It is the utterance of
somebody who, in the words of Kipling, knew the
worst too young; not necessarily in his own act or
by his own fault, but by the nature of a system which
saw no difference between the worst and the moder-
ately bad. But whatever form the shock of evil might
take, I think it jerked him out of the right development of his romantic nature; and was responsible for
much that seemed random or belated in his life.

I do not mean to imply that the morality of the
story itself has anything of weakness or morbidity;
my opinion is very much the other way. Though the
fable may seem mad, the moral is very sane; indeed,
the moral is strictly orthodox. The trouble is that
most of those who mention it do not know the moral,
possibly because they have never read the fable. From

time to time those anonymous authorities in the newspapers, who dismiss Stevenson with such languid grace, will say that there is something quite cheap and obvious about the idea that one man is really two men and can be divided into the evil and the good. Unfortunately for them, that does not happen to be the idea. The real stab of the story is not in the discovery that the one man is two men; but in the discovery that the two men are one man. After all the diverse wandering and warring of those two incompatible beings, there was still one man born and only one man buried. Jekyll and Hyde have become a proverb and a joke; only it is a proverb read backwards and a joke that nobody really sees. But it might have occurred to the languid critics, as a part of the joke, that the tale is a tragedy; and that this is only another way of saying that the experiment was a failure. The point of the story is not that a man *can* cut himself off from his conscience, but that he cannot. The surgical operation is fatal in the story. It is an amputation of which both the parts die. Jekyll, even in dying, declares the conclusion of the matter; that the load of man's moral struggle is bound upon him and cannot be thus escaped. The reason is that there can never be equality between the evil and the good. Jekyll and Hyde are not twin brothers. They are

[54]

rather, as one of them truly remarks, like father and son. After all, Jekyll created Hyde; Hyde would never have created Jekyll; he only destroyed Jekyll. The notion is not so hackneyed as the critics find it, after Stevenson has found it for them thirty years ago. But Jekyll's claim is not that it is the first of such experiments in duality; but rather that it must be the last.

Nor do I necessarily admit the technical clumsiness which some have alleged against the tale, merely because I believe that many of its emotions were first experienced in the crude pain of youth. Some have gone into particular detail in order to pick it to pieces; and Mr. E. F. Benson has made the (to me) strange remark that the structure of the story breaks down when Jekyll discovers that his chemical combination was partly accidental and is therefore unrecoverable. The critic says scornfully that it would have done just as well if Jekyll had taken a blue pill. It seems to me odd that any one who seems to know so much about the devil as the author of *Colin* should fail to recognise the cloven hoof in the cloven spirit called up by the Jekyll experiment. That moment in which Jekyll finds his own formula fail him, through an accident he had never foreseen, is simply the supreme moment in every story of a man buying power from hell; the moment when he finds the flaw in the deed. Such a moment comes to Macbeth and Faustus and a hundred others; and the whole point of it is that nothing is really secure, least of all a Satanist security. The moral is that the devil is a liar, and more especially a traitor; that he is more dangerous to his friends than his foes; and, with all deference to Mr. Benson, it is not a shallow or unimportant moral. But although the story ultimately emerged as a gargoyle very carefully graven by a mature master-craftsman, and was moreover a gargoyle of the greatest spiritual edification, eminently suited to be stuck on to the most sacred edifice, my point for the moment is that the stone of which it was made was originally found, I think, by Stevenson as a boy, kicking about the street, not to mention the gutter. In other words, he did not need to leave the respectable metropolis of the north to find the weaknesses of Jekyll and the crimes of Hyde.

I deal with these things in general terms, not merely out of delicacy, but partly out of something that I might almost call impatience or contempt. For the quarrels between the Victorian whitewashers and the Post-Victorian mudslingers seem to me deficient in the ordinary decent comprehension of the difficulties of human nature. Both the scandalised and the scandalmonger seem to me to look very silly beside the sensible person in the Bible, who confined himself to saying that there are things that no man knows, such as the way of a bird in the air and the way of a man in his youth. That Stevenson was in the mature and sane sense a good man is certain, without any Victorian apologetics; that he never did anything that he thought wrong is improbable, even without any elaborate cloacan researches; and the whole thing is further falsified by the fact that, outside a certain religious tradition, very few either of the whitewashers or the mudslingers really believe in the morality involved. The former seek to save nothing better than respectability; the latter even when they slander can hardly condemn. Stevenson was not a Catholic: he did not pretend to have remained a Puritan; but he was a highly honourable, responsible and chivalrous Pagan, in a world of Pagans who were most of them considerably less conspicuous for chivalry and honour. I for one, if I may say so, am ready to defend my own standards or to judge other men by theirs. But the Victorian pretence that every well-dressed hero of romance with over five hundred a year is born immune from the temptations which the mightiest saints have rolled themselves in brambles to control—that does not concern me and I shall not discuss it again.

But what does concern me, at this particular stage of the story, is not the question of what Stevenson thought right or wrong when he had become consciously and consistently a Pagan, but the particular way in which right and wrong appeared to him at this crude and groping age when he was still by tradition a Puritan. And I do think there was something tail-foremost, to use one of his own favourite words, in the way in which evil crept into his existence, as it does into everybody else's. He saw the tail of the devil before he saw his horns. Puritanism gave him the key rather to the cellars than the halls of Babylon; and something thus subterranean, suffocating and debased rolls like a smoke over the story of Jekyll and Hyde. But I only mention these matters as part of a general unfolding of his mind and moral nature, which seems to me to have had a great deal to do with the latter development of his destiny. The normal, or at least the ideal, development of a man's destiny is from the coloured chamber of childhood to an even more romantic garden of the faith and tryst of youth. It is from the child's garden of verses to the man's garden of vows. I do not think that time of transition went right with Stevenson; I think that something thwarted or misled him; I think it was then that the east wind of Edinburgh Puritanism blew him out of his course, so that he returned only long after to anything like a secure loyalty and a right human relation. In a word, I think that in his childhood he had the best luck in the world, and in his youth the worst luck in the world; and that this explains most of his story.

Anyhow, he found no foothold on those steep streets of his beautiful and precipitous city; and as he looked forth over the litter of little islands in the large and shining estuary, he may have had some foreshadowing of that almost vagabond destiny which ended in the ends of the earth. There seemed in one sense no social reason why it should not end in Edinburgh as it had begun in Edinburgh. There seemed nothing against a normal successful career for one so brilliant, so graceful and essentially so humane; his story might have been as comfortable as a Victorian three-volume novel. He might have had the luck to marry an Edinburgh lady as delightful and satisfactory as Barbara Grant. He might have presided over the revels of a new bunch of Stevensons, coming home from Leith Walk laden with the gay portfolios of Skelt. They also might have bought Penny Pickwicks or gone about girt with lanterns; and his own view of these things might have altered, though not necessarily weakened, with the responsibility of one who sees them reproduced in others. But among these early Edinburgh pranks, which he has left on record, was one which is something of a symbol. He speaks somewhere of a special sort of apples which he gathered by the seashore, which were such as might well be gathered from the salted and crooked trees that grow by the sea. I do not know what it was; or what form it took; or whether it ever took any definable form at all. But somehow or other, in thought or word or deed, in that bleak place he ate the apple of knowledge; and it was a crab apple.

I think it was partly the pains of youth that afterwards made so vivid to him the pleasures of childhood. The break in his life was of course partly due to the break in his health. But it was also due, I think, to something ragged and unseemly in the edge of life he laid hold of when he touched the hem of her garment; to something unsatisfactory in all that side of existence as it appears accidentally to the child of Puritan conventions. The effect on him was that, during those years, he grew up too much out of touch with his domestic and civic, if not his national traditions; knowing at once too much and too little. He was never denationalised; for he was a Scotsman; and a Scotsman never is, even when he is in theory internationalised. But he did begin to become internationalised, in the sense that he gained a sort of indiscriminate intimacy with the culture of the world, especially the rather cynical sort of culture which was then current. The local and domestic conventions, which were in many ways wrong, lost their power to control him even when they were right. And in all that retrospect nothing remained so real as the unreal romances of the first days. In the Puritan creeds there was nothing that he could believe, even as much as he had believed in make-believe. There was nothing to call him back half so clearly as the call of that childish rhyme of which he afterwards wrote, in the touching dedication that has the burden, "How far is it to Babylon?" Unfortunately it is not very far to Babylon. That cosmopolitan market of the arts, which is in his story perhaps best represented by Paris, called to him more and more to live the life of the complete artist, which in those days had something like a touch of the complete anarchist. He passed into it, ultimately in person and already in spirit; there was nothing to call him back but the thin and tiny cry of a tin trumpet; that sounded once and was mute.

I say there was nothing to call him back; and very little to restrain him; and to any one who really understands the psychology and philosophy of that time of transition, it is really rather a wonder that he was so restrained. All his after adventures will be misunderstood if we do not realise that he left behind him a dead religion. Men are misled by the fact that he often used the old national creed as a subject; which really means rather that it had become an object. It was a subject that had ceased to be subjective; he worked upon it and not with it. He and the inheritors of his admirable tradition, like Barrie and Buchan, treated that national secret genially and even tenderly; but their very tenderness was the first soft signal that the thing was dead. At least they would never have so fondled the tiger-cat of Calvinism until, for them, its teeth were drawn. Indeed this was the irony and the pathos of the position of Scottish Calvinism: to be rammed down people's throats for three hundred years as an unanswerable argument and then to be inherited at the last as an almost indefensible affection; to be expounded to boys with a scowl and remembered by men with a smile; to crush down all human sentiments and to linger at last in the sentimental comedy of Thrums. All that long agony of lucidity and masterful logic ended at last suddenly with a laugh; and the laugh was Robert Louis Stevenson. With him the break had come; and it follows that something in himself was broken. The whaups were crying round the graves of the martyrs, and his heart remembered, but not his mind; great Knox blew thrice upon the trumpet, and what thrilled him were no words but a noise; Old Mortality seemed still to be tinkering on his eternal round to preserve the memorials of the Covenant, but a bell had already tolled to announce that even Old Mortality was mortal. When Stevenson stepped into the wider world of the Continent, with its more graceful logic and even its more graceful vice, he went as one emptied of all the ethics and metaphysics of his home, and open to all the views and vices of a rationalistic civilisation. All the deeper lessons of his early life must have seemed to him to be dead within him; nor did he himself know what thing within him was yet alive.

THE REACTION TO ROMANCE

CHAPTER IV

THE REACTION TO ROMANCE

WHEN a man walks down the street with a very long feather stuck in his hat and streaming behind him, or carrying a gold-hilted rapier cocked at a gallant angle, there are some among the typists and clerks of Clapham Junction shrewd enough to perceive that there is something faintly ostentatious about him. And when a man walks down Piccadilly or the parade at Bournemouth with long hair streaming behind him and surmounted by an embroidered smoking-cap, there are not wanting critics so acute as to deduce (with all the detailed shrewdness of Sherlock Holmes) that such a man is not entirely averse from being looked at. Many long and laborious studies of Stevenson have been published lately, to fortify and establish this remarkable result; and I need not devote myself to proving it further. Let us record with all due solemnity that Robert Louis Stevenson has been convicted by the court of being very vain, if "dressing up" in the manner of a child, and not resenting the consequent conspicuous position, be the marks of vanity. But there is one aspect of this truth which seems to me to have been strangely and even astonishingly overlooked. Everybody talks as if Stevenson had been not only conspicuous but quite unique in this sort of vanity. Everybody seems to assume that among the artists of his time he was entirely alone in his affectation. Contrasting in this respect with the humdrum respectability of Oscar Wilde, notable as the very reverse of the evangelical meekness of Jimmy Whistler, standing out as he does against the stodgy chapel-going piety of Max Beerbohm, having none of the cheery commonplaces of Aubrey Beardsley or the prosaic self-effacement of Richard Le Gallienne, he naturally aroused attention by the slightest deviation into oddity or dandyism; things notoriously so unpopular among the decadents of the 'nineties. Among other things, everybody seems to have forgotten that Stevenson lived for some time among the Parisian art students; who have never been remarkable for the bourgeois regularity of their coats and hats. Yet he actually mentions the offensive smoking-cap himself as originating in the Bohemian masquerade of the Quartier Latin. There he was not so much being eccentric as being conventional; for the convention was unconventionality. A mob of men in that place and at that age, would have played the

[68]

same sort of tricks and worn the same kind of clothes; nor was Stevenson, as I have said, the only one of them who carried these attitudes and antics through life. Any one of them might have worn a smoking-cap; none of them would have objected to any variety of fool's cap, though they hardly wished it identified with a dunce's cap. Many of them, still alive, would cheerfully admit that the cap fits. But poor Stevenson is to be remembered as a fool, because all the fools are forgotten except Stevenson.

It was not that sort of oddity that was really odd. The costume for which he is now conspicuous was really part of a carnival. The attitude in which he stands, to the astonishment and grief of the critics, was really the fashion of a crowd. But what was really individual and interesting about him was the way in which he did actually react against the surroundings; the point at which he refused to run with the crowd or follow the fashion. No insanity in that cheerful lunatic asylum is so interesting to the psychologist as the shock of Stevenson going sane. No romantic ruffianism in which he may or may not have indulged is so curious as the real spirit of his revolt into respectability.

Treasure Island, if hardly a historical novel, was essentially a historical event. The rise or revolt of

R. L. S. must be taken in relation to history, to the history of the whole European mind and mood. It was, first and last, a reaction against pessimism. There was thrown across all that earth and sky the gigantic shadow of Schopenhauer. At least it seemed gigantic then, though some of us may already have suspected that the shadow was larger than the man. Anyhow, in that period we might almost say that pessimism was another name for culture. Cheerfulness was associated with the Philistine, like the broad grin with the bumpkin. Pessimism could be read between the lines of the lightest triolet or most elegant essay. Any one who really remembers that time will admit that the world was much more hopeful after the worst of its wars than it was not long before. Mr. H. G. Wells, whose genius had just been discovered by Henley, was very much older than he is now. He was prophesying that the outline of history would end, not in communism, but in cannibalism. He was prophesying the end of the world: a crack of doom not even cheerful enough to be a day of judgement. Oscar Wilde, who perhaps filled up more room, both in mind and body, than anybody else on that stage at that moment, expressed his philosophy in that bitter parable in which Christ seeks to comfort a man weeping and

is answered, "Lord, I was dead and you raised me to
life; what else can I do but weep?"

This was the spirit that was behind all that levity;
a levity that was like fireworks in more ways than
one. We talk of some Whistlerian satire as a squib;
but squibs can only shine in the dark. It is all the difference between the colours of fireworks that have
their back to the vault of night and the colours of
church windows that have their backs to the sun.
For these people all the light of life was in the fore-
ground; there was nothing in the background but an
abyss. They were rather nihilists than atheists; for
there is a difference between worshipping Nothing
and not worshipping anything. Now the interest of the
next stage of Stevenson is that he stood up suddenly
amid all these things and shook himself with a sort of
impatient sanity; a shrug of scepticism about scepticism. His real distinction is that he had the sense to
see that there is nothing to be done with Nothing.
He saw that in that staggering universe it was abso-
lutely necessary to stand somehow on something; and
instead of falling about anyhow with all the other
lunatics, he did seek for a ledge on which he could
really stand. He did definitely and even dramatically
refuse to go mad; or, what is very much worse, to re-

main futile. But the whole turning-point of the tale is now missed; partly by the too concentrated idolatry of the sentimentalists, and partly by the too concentrated spite of the iconoclasts. They miss the *historic* relation of the man to his time and school. It was one of the crowd of artists who showed mutinous signs of deserting art for life. It was even one of the decadents who refused to decay.

Now what really remains interesting in this story of Stevenson, in spite of all the vain repetitions, is the authority to which he appealed. It was rather an odd one; and many would have said that his sanity was madder than madness. He did not appeal to any ideal of the sort usually pursued by idealists; he did not try to construct an optimist philosophy like Spinoza or Emerson; he did not preach a good time coming like William Morris or Wells; he did not appeal to Imperialism or Socialism or Scotland: he appealed to Skelt.

Familiarity had dulled the divine paradox that we should learn morality from little children. He advanced the more disturbing paradox that we should learn morality from little boys. The young child who should lead us was the common (or garden) little boy: the boy of the catapult and the toy pistol—and the toy theatre. Stevenson seemed to say to the semi-suicides drooping round him at the café tables; drinking absinthe and discussing atheism: "Hang it all, the hero of a penny-dreadful play was a better man than you are! A Penny Plain and Twopence Coloured was an art more worthy of living men than the art that you are all professing. Painting pasteboard figures of pirates and admirals was better worth doing than all this, it was fun; it was fighting; it was a life and a lark; and if I can't do anything else, dang me but I will try to do that again!" So was presented to the world this entertaining spectacle; of the art student surrounded by easels on which other artists were debating the fine shades of Corot and Renoir, while he himself was gravely painting mariners a bright prussian blue of a shilling paint-box and shedding their blood in streams of unmistakable crimson lake. That is the primary paradox about Stevenson's early manhood; or, if you will, the real joke about Stevenson. Of all that intellectualism in Bohemia the result was the return to Skelt. Of all that wallowing in Balzac the remarkable outcome was *Treasure Island*. But it is no exaggeration to say that it had still more to do with toys than treasures. Stevenson was not really looking forward or outward to a world of larger things, but backward and inward into a world of smaller ones: in the peepshow of Skelt, which was still the true window of the world.

Thus, Skelt and his puppets seemed made for a repartee to the favourite phrases of the pessimists. All that world was haunted as with melody by the hedonist despair of Fitzgerald's Omar: one of the great historical documents of this history. No image could make them bow their heads with more hopelessness and helplessness of despair than that famous one:

> "We are none other than a moving row
>   Of magic shadow-shapes that come and go
>   Around the sun-illumined lantern held
>   At midnight by the Master of the show."

And no image could make the infant Stevenson kick his little legs with keener joy. His answer, in effect, to the philosophy of the magic shadow-shapes, was that the shadow-shapes really were magic. At any rate, they really did seem to the children to be magic: and it was not false but true psychology to call the thing a magic lantern. He was capable of feeling passionate delight in being such a Lantern-Bearer. He was capable even of feeling passionate delight in being such a shadow. And any one who has seen a shadow pantomime as a child, as I have, and who has retained any living link with his own childhood, will realise that Omar was as unlucky in his commentary on the lantern-show as the delightful curate in *Voces Populi* who talked about Valentine and Orson. He was teaching optimism as an illustration to pessimism. Later we may make a guess at the nature of this glamour about such tricks or toys; the point for the moment is that they were associated with gloom in philosophy, while they were associated with pleasure in psychology. The same applies to more common examples of the fancies of the fatalist. When the sage said that men are "only puppets," it must have seemed to the young Louis almost like the blasphemy of saying they were "only pirates." It might well seem to any child like saying that they were only fairies. There was something weak about bewailing drearily the fate of the puppets of destiny, to an audience that was eagerly awaiting the joyful apocalypse of a puppet-show. The Stevensonian reaction might be roughly represented by the suggestion—if we are as futile as puppets, is there anything particular to prevent our being as entertaining as Punch? And there is, as I say, a real spiritual mystery behind this mystical ecstasy of mimicry. If living dolls were so dull and dead, why in the world were dead dolls so very much alive? And if being a puppet is so depressing, how is it that the puppet of a puppet can be so enthralling?

It is to be noted that this sort of romanticism, as compared with realism, is *not* more superficial, but on the contrary more fundamental. It is an appeal from what is experienced to what is felt. When people are avowedly talking about happiness and unhappiness, as the pessimists were, it is futile to say that shadows and sham pasteboard figures *ought* not to make people happy. It was futile to tell the young Stevenson that the toy-theatre shop was a dingy booth stocked with dusty rolls of paper, covered with ill-drawn and ungainly figures; and to insist that these were the only facts. He naturally answered: "My facts were my feelings; and what do you make of those facts? Either there is something in Skelt; which you do not admit. Or else there is something in Life; which you also do not admit." Hence arose that answer to the realists which is best expressed in the essay called *The Lantern-Bearers*. The realists, who overlook so many details, have never quite noticed where lay the falsity of their method; it lay in the fact that so long as it was materialistic, it could not really be realistic. For it could not be psychological. If toys and trifles can make people happy, that happiness is not a trifle and certainly cannot be a trick.

This is the point that has been missed in all the talk about posing. Those who repeat for the hundredth time that he posed have not got as far as the obvious question, "Posed as what?" All the other poets and artists posed; but they posed as the members of the Suicide Club. He posed as Prince Florizel with a sword, challenging the President of the Suicide Club. He was, if you will, the foolish masker I have imagined, tricked out with a feather and a sword or dagger; but not tricked out more extravagantly than those who appeared as fantastic figures at their own funeral. If he had a feather, it was not a white feather; if he had a dagger, it was not a poisoned dagger or the pessimist dagger that is turned inwards; in short, if he had a posture it was a posture of defence and even of defiance. And it was, after all, the fashionable posture of his time which he set himself to defy. And it is here that it is really relevant to remember that he was not altogether posturing when he said he was defying death. Death was much nearer to him than it was to the pessimists; and he knew it whenever he coughed and found blood on his handkerchief. He was not pretending to defy it half so much as they were pretending to seek it. It is no very unreasonable claim for him that he made a better use of his bad health than Oscar Wilde made of his good health; and nothing affected in the externals of either can alter the contrast. The dagger may have been theatrical; but the blood was real. As Cyrano said of his friend, "Le sang, c'est le sien." And it really was the absence of courage in the current culture that awoke his protest or pose. In any case, the intellectual fine shades were morally more than a little shady. But he hated chiefly the loss of what soldiers call morale rather than what parsons call morality. All that world cowered under the shadow of death. All alike were travelling under the flag of the skull and crossbones. But he alone could call it the Jolly Roger.

What is really not appreciated about Stevenson is the abruptness of this breakaway. We talk of looking back with gratitude to innovators or the introducers of new ideas; but in fact nothing is more difficult to do, since for us they are now necessarily old ideas. There is only one moment, at most, of triumph for the original thinker; while his thought is an originality and before it becomes merely an origin. News spreads quickly; that is, it grows stale quickly; and though we may call a work wonderful, we cannot easily put ourselves in the position of those for whom it was a cause of wonder, in the sense of surprise. Between the first fashion of talking too much in praise of Stevenson, and the newer fashion of talking nonsense in disparagement of Stevenson, we have become quite familiar with the association of certain ideas; of extreme stylistic polish applied to rough schoolboy adventure, of the Penny Plain figure tinted as carefully as a miniature. But these ideas were not always associated in the way in which Stevenson associated them. We may tear the combination to pieces, but it was he who wove it together; and—as many would have thought—of very incongruous threads. It really did seem preposterous to many that a serious literary artist of the age of Pater should devote himself to rewriting Penny Dreadfuls. It was just as if George Meredith had chosen to put all his fine feminine psychology into writing the sort of twopenny novelettes that were read by housemaids, and called "Pansy's Elopement" or "Winnie's Wedding Bells." It was as if Henry James had been heard to say or, so to speak, to suggest, that there was, after all, and in a way quite annoyingly overlooked, *something*—something that really should have been better evaluated and re-expressed, as it were, in all that really unquestionable productiveness of *Ally Sloper's Half-Holiday*. It was as if Paderewski had insisted on only going round with a barrel-organ; or Whistler had confined himself solely to painting public-house signs. A distinguished dramatist, who is old enough to remember in his youth the first successes of Stevenson's manhood, told me how absurd it seemed at the time that any one should take seriously such gutter literature of the *gamin*. A book written only for boys generally meant a book written only for errand-boys. It seemed a strange association of ideas that it should be written carefully as a book for men, and even for literary men. It does not seem so strange now; because Stevenson has done it quite a long time ago. But it is important to realise that not everybody thought it natural to expend the style of *Pulvis et Umbra* on the equivalent of "Dick Deadshot Among the Pirates." It was the very last sort of enthusiasm that would have easily carried any of his cultivated contemporaries off their feet. The typical literary man, with the outlook and philosophy of that generation, would have been about as likely to pass his life in throwing paper darts or chalking caricatures of his publisher on a blackboard.

Thus, there is one of those phrases quoted too much, as against so many quoted too little, that he and his artistic friends bore with them bulky yellow volumes "quite impudently French." But, by the tests of that artistic world, *Treasure Island* is quite impudently English. By the conventions of that world, there was nothing unconventional about studying Balzac or being Bohemian. It was much more unconventional to study Captain Marryat and to write about the good captain who flew the Union Jack over the stockade, in defiance of the bad buccaneers. From the standpoint of Art in those days, even that flag was a much too Moral Emblem. It is only when we understand what there was that seemed quaint and even undignified in his adventurous antic, that we can clearly understand the unconscious truths that lay behind it. For, as against the black flag of pessimism, his flag really was a Moral Emblem. There was a morality in his reaction into adventure; his appeal to the spirit of the highway—though it were sometimes the spirit of the highwayman.

In other words, he appealed to his own childhood. A tale is told of it: that when some one chaffed him about a toy sword he replied solemnly, "The hilt is of gold and the scabbard of silver and the child is well content." It was to that moment that he suddenly returned. Groping for something that would satisfy, he found nothing so solid as that fancy. That had not been Nothing; that had not been pessimistic; that was not a life over which Lazarus could do nothing but weep. That was as positive as the paints in the paint-box and the difference between vermilion and chrome yellow. Its pleasures had been as solid as the taste of sweets; and it was nonsense to say that there had been nothing in them worth living for. Play at least is always serious. So long as we can say, "Let us pretend," we must be sincere. Therefore he appealed across the void or valley of his somewhat sterile youth to that garden of childhood, which he had once known and which was his nearest notion of paradise. There were no shrines in the faith or in the city of his fathers; there were no channels of consecration or confession; there was no imagery save in the faceless images left behind by the image-breakers. A man in his mood of reaction towards happiness might almost as well have prayed to the Black Man who figured as the Scottish provincial devil as to the God behind the black cloud that sent out such stiff horrific rays in the Calvinist family Bible. But in all that waste of Scottish moorland, the sun still glowed on that square of garden like a patch of gold. The lessons were lost, but the toys were eternal; the men had been harsh, but the child had been well content; if there were nothing better, he would return.

In the elementary philosophy of the thing, of course, what moved Stevenson was what moved

Wordsworth; the unanswerable fact of that first vividness in the vision of life. But he had it in his own
quaint way; and it was hardly the vision of meadow,
grove and stream. It was rather the vision of coffin,
gallows and gory sabre that were apparelled in celes-
tial light, the glory and the freshness of a dream. But
he was appealing to a sort of sanguinary innocence
against a sort of silent and secretive perversion. Here,
as everywhere in this rude outline, I am taking a
thing like *Treasure Island,* in a spirit of simplification and symbol. I do not mean, of course, that he
wrote *Treasure Island* sitting in a café on the boule-
vards; any more than I mean that he wrote *Jekyll
and Hyde* in a cellar or a garret in the lands of the
Cowgate. Both these books were developed by stages
of the greatest literary care, in later life; and pursued with the characteristic consistency of his art
through all the equally characteristic mutability of
his domicile. When I say that a certain book came
out of a certain experience, I mean that he drew on
that experience to write it, or that it was the ulti-
mate result of the reaction which that experience
produced in his mind. And I mean in this case that
what shaped and sharpened Stevenson's memory of
the mere nonsense of Skeltery was his growing sense
of the need of some escape from the suffocating cyn-

icism of the mass of men and artists in his time. He wished to go back to that nonsense; for it seemed, by comparison, quite sensible.

Treasure Island was written as a boy's book; perhaps it is not always read as a boy's book. I sometimes fancy that a real boy could read it better if he could read it backwards. The end, which is full of skeletons and ancient crime, is in the fullest sense beautiful; it is even idealistic. For it is the realisation of an ideal, that which is promised in its provocative and beckoning map; a vision not only of white skeletons but also green palm trees and sapphire seas. But the beginning of the book, considered as a boy's book, can hardly be called idealistic; and is found in practice to be rather too realistic. I may make an egotistical confession here, which I think is not unique and not without its universal inference about the spirit of youth. When I read the book as a child, I was not horrified by what are called the horrors. Something did indeed shock me, just a little more than a child should be shocked; for of course he would have no fun if he were never shocked at all. But what shook me was not the dead man's chest or the live man's crimes or the information that "Drink and the devil have done for the rest"; all that seemed to me quite cheery and comforting. What did seem to me ugly was exactly what might happen in any inn-parlour, if there were no pirates in the world. It was that business about apoplexy; or some sort of alcoholic poisoning. It was the sailor having a mysterious thing called a stroke; so much more terrifying than any sabre-stroke. I was ready to wade in seas of gore; for all that gore was crimson lake; and indeed I always imagined it as a lake of crimson. Exactly what I was not ready for were those few drops of blood drawn from the arm of the insensible sailor, when he was bled by the surgeon. That blood is not crimson lake. Thus we have the paradox that I was horrified by the act of healing; while all the rowdy business of hitting and hurting did not hurt me at all. I was disgusted with an act of mercy, because it took the form of medicine. I will not pause to draw the many morals of this paradox; especially in relation to a common fallacy of pacifism. I will content myself with saying, whether I make my meaning clear or no, that a child is not wicked enough to disapprove of war.

But whatever be the case with most boys, there was certainly one boy who enjoyed *Treasure Island;* and his name was Robert Louis Stevenson. He really had very much of the feeling of one who had got away to great waters and outlandish lands; perhaps even more vividly than he had it later, when he made that voyage not metaphorically but materially, and found his own Treasure Island in the South Seas. But just as in the second case he was fleeing to clear skies from unhealthy climates, so he was in reviving the adventure story escaping from an exceedingly unhealthy climate. The microbe of morbidity may have been within him, as well as the germ of phthisis; but in the cities he had left behind pessimism was raging like a pestilence. Multitudes of pale-faced poets, formless and forgotten, sat crowded at those café tables like ghosts in Hades, worshipping "la sorcière glauque," like that one of them whose mortality has been immortalised by Max. It is too often forgotten that if Stevenson had really been only a pale young man making wax flowers, he would have found plenty of pale young men to make them with him; and the flowers and flower-makers would long have withered together. But he alone escaped, as from a city of the dead; he cut the painter as Jim Hawkins stole the boat, and went on his own voyage, following the sun. Drink and the devil have done for the rest, especially the devil; but then they were drinking absinthe and not with a "Yo ho ho"; consuming it without the most feeble attempt at any "Yo ho ho"—a defect which was, of course, the most serious and important part of the affair. For "Yo ho ho" was precisely what Stevenson, with his exact choice of words, particularly desired to say just then. It was for the present his most articulate message to mankind.

THE SCOTTISH STORIES

CHAPTER V

THE SCOTTISH STORIES

PROVERBS are generally true, when they are the proverbs of the people; so long as they are not proverbs about another people. It was unwise to search Sussex to discover if Kentish men had tails, or England to learn if French husbands had horns. And obviously there is much that is misleading in the traditional type of the practical Puritanical Scotsman, with his dry thrift and bleak respectability. A figure of such severe decorum is not very vividly evoked either by the title of Rab the Ranter or the Wizard of the North. And few of our own generation are yet convinced of it, even by the scientific severity that has given us *Peter Pan* or the sober responsibility that stiffens the narrative of *The New Arabian Nights*. The readers of the latter work will be much interested to realise that a Scotsman is incapable of seeing a joke, since he seems so eminently capable of making one; and the reader of the former will be disposed to suggest that the national jesting is not too sober but rather too extravagant. *Peter Pan* carries on by

lineal tradition the cult of the child, beginning with
Treasure Island; but if there be anything to criticise
in Sir James Barrie's beautiful fantasia, it is that
wilder things happen to Wendy in a London nursery
than ever happened to Jim in a tropical island. The
only object to living in a nursery where the dog is
the nurse, or the father lives in the dog-kennel, is
that there seems no necessity to go to the Never-
Never Land to look for the things that never happen.
Whatever else we say of the Scottish genius, it is
certainly not merely dry or prosaic; and indeed the
real mixture of the Scottish genius is as full of con-
tradictions as that pattern of crosses in the Scottish
plaid. And even here there is subtlety as well as cross-
purposes; and the tartan may be an old tribal form
of camouflage.

There is an aspect of a Scottish hill or moor, which
for the moment will look grey and at the least change
of light look purple; which is in itself an image of
Scotland. A passing from the most dispassionate to
the most passionate tint, which yet seems to be no
more than a new shade, might well represent the
mixture of restraint and violence that runs through
the national history and the national character. Stevenson stands for one of those moments in the national history when the grey turned to purple; and

yet in his purple there is still a great deal of grey.
There is a great deal of restraint, artistic even more
than moral; there is a certain coolness in the commentary even on picturesque objects; there is even
a certain absence of the common conception of passion. There are shades even in purple; there are differences between the purple orchid and the purple
heather; and his often seems to be like white heather,
for luck. In other words, his idea of happiness is still
of the breezy and boyish sort; and though he described the happiness of lovers very happily in *Catriona* and began to foreshadow their unhappiness in
Weir of Hermiston, he attacked the theme relatively
late in life; and it counted for little in that original
idea of a return to simplicity, which had come upon
him like a wind from a playground. Imagine how
annoyed Jim Hawkins would have been, if a lot of
girls had been allowed to muck up the business of
going after treasure! So brilliant is this resurrection
of boyhood, that we almost believe for the moment
that Stevenson must have been as young and callous
as Jim. Only I suspect, as I say, that in some ways he
had even made himself a little callous in those matters. There his adventures had been misadventures.
He did not recall for mere pleasure the memory of
youth, as he did the memory of boyhood.

[93]

The two novels about David Balfour are very notable examples of what I have mentioned generally as the Stevensonian note; the brisk and bright treatment, the short speeches, the sharp gestures and the pointed profile of energy, as of a man following his nose very rapidly along the open road. The great scenes in *Kidnapped,* the defence of the Round House or the confrontation of Uncle Ebenezer and Alan Breck, are full of those snapping phrases that seem to pick things off like pistol shots. A whole essay on the style of Stevenson, such as I shall attempt forlornly and ineffectually on another page, might be written by a real critic on the phrase, "His sword flashed like quicksilver into the huddle of our fleeing enemies." The fact that the name of a certain metal happens to combine the word "silver" with the word "quick" is simply a rather recondite accident; but the art of Stevenson consisted in taking advantage of such accidents. To those who say that such tricks are easy to play or such words easy to find, the only answer is, "Go and find them." An author cannot create words, unless he be the happy author of *Jaberwocky* or *The Land Where the Jumblies Live;* but the nearest he can come to creating them is finding them in such a fashion and for such a use. The characters in the story are excellent, though perhaps there are really only two of them. There are more in the sequel called *Catriona;* and the study of the Lord Advocate Prestongrange is a highly interesting attempt to do a very difficult thing; to describe a politician who has not altogether ceased to be a man. The dialogue is spirited and full of fine Scottish humours, but all these things are almost as secondary in *Kidnapped* and *Catriona* as they are in *Treasure Island* itself. The thing is still simply an adventure story, and especially a boy's adventure story; such as is fitted to describe the adventures of a boy. And there are moments when it is the same boy; and his name is neither Hawkins nor Balfour, but Stevenson.

But though the thing is to be criticised (and admired) strictly as an adventure story, there are sidelights of interest about it considered as a historical novel. It carries on a rather curiously balanced critical attitude, partly inherited from the attitude of Sir Walter Scott; the paradox of being intellectually on the side of the Whigs and morally on the side of the Jacobites. There is enough moral material, in the story of the long legal murder of James of the Glens, to raise a whole clan of Jacobites and roll them redhot down the pass of Killiecrankie. But there still stands over against it the large legal assumption that in some sort of way all these things will be for the best, which is the inheritance of the providential view of the Presbyterian settlement. Similarly, it is obvious in the earlier story that David Balfour does not really differ very much from Alan Breck, in his view of the oppression of the Highland crofters and their pathetic loyalty to the past. In the ethical balance of the Appin Murder, if he does not palliate tyrannicide, he certainly says nothing calculated to palliate tyranny. It is obvious that he is moved and impressed with the spectacle of a whole peasantry loyal to their ideal and defying a more civilised but a much more cynical pressure. But, curiously enough, when Stevenson saw exactly the same story acted before his eyes in the tragedy of the peasants of Ireland, he was carried away by some newspaper nonsense about the wickedness of the Land League (prodded perhaps by the rather absurd Jingoism of Henley) and, with all his native courage and much less than his native sense, wanted to plant himself on an eviction farm belonging to a family named Curtin, whom he seemed to regard as the sole victims of the social situation. It did not seem to occur to him that he was merely assisting the Master of Lovat to bully David Balfour. He seemed really to suppose that, in those social conditions, the Irish peasants could look for justice to imperial governments which abolished all local rights and carried away every Irish patriot to be tried before a packed jury of foreigners and foes. "Justice, David! The same justice, by all the world, that Glenure found by the roadside."

But this curious and sometimes inconsistent mingling of the grey Whiggery with the purple Jacobite romance, in the traditional sentiment of such Scots as Stevenson, is connected with much deeper things touching the hold that their history had upon them. It is necessary to state at this stage that there is really and seriously an influence of Scottish Puritanism upon Stevenson; though I think it rather a philosophy partially accepted by his intellect than the special ideal that was the secret of his heart. But every philosopher is affected by philosophy; even if, as in the immortal instance in Boswell, cheerfulness is always breaking out. And there was a part of Stevenson's mind that was not cheerful; which I think, in some manifestations, was not even healthy. And yet the tribute of truth is due to that special Scottish element; that even when we say it was not healthy, we can hardly venture to say it was not strong. It was the shadow of that ancient heathen fatalism, which in the seventeenth century had taken the hardly less heathen form of Calvinism; and which had sounded in so many Scottish tragedies with a note of doom. We appreciate it sharply when we turn from his two Scottish comedies of adventure to his third Scottish romance, which is a tragedy of character. It is true, as may be noted later, that even into this concentrated drama of sin and sorrow there enters a curious and rather incongruous element of the adventure story; like a fragment of the former adventures of David or Jim. But leaving that aside for the moment, we must do justice to the dignity which is given to the story itself by its more sombre scenery and its sterner creed. Stevenson showed his perfect instinct when he called it *A Winter's Tale*. It is his one story in black and white, and I cannot recall one word that is a patch of colour.

In touching on the rather neglected point of the nastier side of Puritan sociology, the raw and barbarous flavour about its evil and excess, I may have seemed to underrate the higher though harsher aspects of Scottish Puritanism. I do not mean to do so; and certainly nobody can afford to do so in attempting an adequate study of Stevenson. He remained to the day of his death in some ways particularly loyal to the Presbyterian tradition; I might say to the Presbyterian prejudices; and at least in one or two cases to the Presbyterian antipathies. But I think it was mostly rather a case of the modern religion of patriotism, as against the larger patriotism of religion. Like many other men of frank, tart and humorous prejudices (which are the sort of prejudices that need never prejudice us against a man) he was apt to see in some foreign things the evils to which he had grown accustomed in native things; and to start again the great international dispute of the pot and the kettle. It is amusing, for instance, to find the young Scotsman in *Olalla* gravely disapproving of the grim Spanish crucifix, with its tortured and grimacing art; and presumably leaving that land of religious gloom, to go back and enjoy the charm and gaiety of *Thrawn Janet*. If there was ever grim and grimacing art, one would think it was in that twisted figure; and even Stevenson admitted that *Olalla* got more comfort from the crucifix than Janet from the minister; or, I will add, the minister from the ministry. Indeed, stories of this kind are told by Stevenson with a deliberate darkening of the Scottish landscape and exultation in the ferocity of the Scottish creed. But it would be quite a mistake to miss in this a certain genuine national pride running through all the abnormal artistry; and a sense that the strength of the tribal tragedy testifies in a manner to the strength of the tribe.

It might be maintained that the best effect of the

Scotsman's religious training was teaching him to do without his religion. It enabled him to survive as a certain sort of freethinker; one who, unlike his more familiar fellows, is not so intoxicated with freedom as to forget to think. It might be said that among the Scots, so far from a sentimental religiosity taking the place of dogmatic religion (as is generally the case among the English), something like the very opposite had occurred. When the religion was dead, the theology remained: at any rate, the taste for theology remained. It remained because, whatever else it is, theology is at least a form of thought. Stevenson certainly retained this turn of mind long after his beliefs, like those of most of his generation, had been simplified to vanishing point. He was, as Henley said, something of the Shorter Catechist; even when his own Catechism had become shorter still. All this, however, was indubitably a strength to him and his nation; and a real reason for gratitude to their old religious tradition. Those dry Deists and hard-headed Utilitarians who stalked the streets of Glasgow and Edinburgh in the eighteenth and early nineteenth centuries were very obviously the products of the national religious spirit. The Scottish atheists were unmistakable children of the Kirk. And though they often seemed absurdly detached and dehumanised, the world is now rather suffering for want of such dull lucidity. To put it shortly, by being theological they had at least learnt to be logical; and in dropping the Greek prefix as a superfluous trifle they will have the sympathy of many moderns much less logical than themselves. The influence of all this sort of clarity on Stevenson is very clear. It did not happen to be his mission to figure as the metaphysical Scotsman; or draw out his deductions along the lines of logic. But he did always by instinct draw lines that were as hard and clear as those of a mathematical diagram. He himself has made a very luminous and valuable comparison between a geometrical theorem and a work of art. I have had cause to remark again and again, in the course of this sketch, on a certain almost arid decision in the strokes of Stevenson's style. I believe it was due in no small degree to that inheritance of definition, that goes with an inheritance of dogma. What he wrote was not written, as he said scornfully of some literary performance, in sand with a saltspoon; it was at least in the tradition of scriptures cut with steel into stone. This was among the many good things that he got from the spiritual atmosphere of his ancestry. But he got other things as well; though they are less easy to describe and far less easy to command.

From time to time I have insensibly and inevitably fallen into a tone of defending Stevenson, as if he needed defence. And indeed I do think that he needs some defence; though not upon the points in which it is now considered necessary to defend him. I do feel a certain impatience with the petty depreciation of our own time, which seems much more frivolous and far less generous than the boom of a best-seller. I do feel a certain contempt for those who call every phrase affected that happens to be effective; or who charge a man with talking for effect, as if there were anything else to talk for. But I should think it very unfair to revile the revilers of Stevenson, without taking the risk of saying where I think he is, if not to be reviled, at least to be rebuked. There was, I think, a weaker strain in Stevenson; but it is the very opposite of the weakness now generally alleged by critics; indeed it is the very opposite of what they would probably regard as weak. The excuse for it, in so far as it existed to be excused, was in the very direction of that sharp turn which he took in early life, when he turned his back upon the decadents. I have already said, and it can hardly be said too often, that the story of Stevenson was a reaction against an age of pessimism. Now the real objection to being a reactionary is that a reactionary, as such, hardly ever avoids reacting into evil and exaggeration. The opposite of the heresy of pessimism was the twin heresy of optimism. Stevenson was not at all attracted to a placid and pacific optimism. But he did begin to be too much attracted to a sort of insolent and oppressive optimism. The reaction from the idea that what is good is always unsuccessful is the idea that what is good is always victorious. And from that many slide into the worse delusion; that what is victorious is always good.

In the days when Stevenson's ancestors the Covenanters were fighting with the Cavaliers, a fine old Cavalier of the Episcopalian persuasion made a rather interesting remark; that the change he really hated was represented by saying "The Lord" instead of "Our Lord." The latter implied affection, the former only fear; indeed he described the former succinctly as the talk of devils. And this is so far true that the very eloquent language in which the name of "The Lord" has figured has generally been the language of might and majesty and even terror. And there really was implied in it in varying degrees the idea of glorifying God for His greatness rather than His goodness. And again there occurred the natural inversion of ideas. Since the Puritan was content to cry with the Moslem: "God is great," so the descendant of the

Puritan is always a little inclined to cry with the Nietzschean: "Greatness is God." In some of the really evil extremes, this sentiment shaded darkly into a sort of diabolism. In Stevenson it was very faintly present; but it is occasionally felt; and by me (I must confess) felt as a fault. It is faintly felt, for instance, in the next great Scottish romance, *The Master of Ballantrae;* it is felt more definitely, I think, in the last Scottish romance of *Weir of Hermiston.* In the first case, Stevenson said in his correspondence, in a tone that was humorous and healthy enough, that The Master was all he knew of The Devil. I do not in the least object to the The Master being The Devil. But I do object to a subtle subconscious something, which every now and then seems almost to suggest that he is The Lord. I mean The Lord in the vague sense of a certain authority in aristocracy, or even in mere mastery. Perhaps I even dimly feel that there is the distant thunder of The Lord in the very title of The Master.

This thing, however we define it and in whatever degree we admit it, had advanced in several degrees when he wrote the later story. Perhaps it was partly the influence of Henley; who, with all his many generous virtues, certainly had this weakness to the point of hysteria. I mean the loss of the natural reaction of a man against a tyrant. It sometimes takes the form of that least masculine of all vices, the admiration for brutality. It has been much debated whether bullies are always cowards; I am content to remark that the admirers of bullies are always, by the very nature of things, trying to be cowards. If they do not always succeed, it is because they have unconscious virtues restraining that obscene worship: and this was true even of Henley; and far truer of Stevenson. Stevenson had always a training in real courage; for he fought when he was weak. But it cannot be denied that, by a combination of causes, his own revolt against spineless pessimism, the reactionary violence of Henley, but chiefly I think the vague Scottish tradition of a God of mere power and terror, he grew too familiar in his later works with the sort of swaggering cult of fear. I feel it in the character of Weir of Hermiston, or rather in the attitude of everybody else, including the author, towards that character. I do not mind the judge exulting over the game of insulting and hanging somebody; for I know the judge can be baser than the man he hangs. But I do mind the author exulting over it, when I know he is not base at all. The same fine shade of unpleasantness can be found in the last pages of *The Ebb-Tide*. My point might be put crudely by saying that I do not object to the author creating such a loathsome person as Mr. Attwater; but I do rather object to his creating him and not loathing him. It would be truer to put the point in another form; that there would be no objection if he loathed and admired Attwater exactly as he loathed and admired Huish. In a sense he obviously did admire Huish; as it was the very passion of his life to admire courage. But he did not expect anybody to look up to Huish; and there are moments when he seems to think it natural that people should look up to Attwater. This secret idolatry of what a feminine sentiment calls "strength," this was the only lesion in Stevenson's perfect sanity, the only running sore in the normal health of his soul; and even that had come from too violent an effort to be healthy. So he might, poor fellow, have started a hæmorrhage by moving too vigorously on his pillow.

For I am not blaming him for having any such evil, in the sense of having any excess of it. I blame him, being what he was, for having even a touch of it. But I think it is unfortunately certain that he did have a touch of it. There is something almost cruel in thus tracing the innocent springs of cruelty. But, as has been said so often and so foolishly and so truly, Robert Louis Stevenson was a child. It is the moral of these chapters about his nation, his city and his home, that he was also something more than a child. He was a lost child. There was nothing to guide him in the mad movements and reactions of modernity; neither his nation nor his religion nor his irreligion were equal to the task. He had no chart for that gallant voyage; he was hardly to blame if he thought he had to choose between the savage rock of the pride of Scylla and the suicidal whirlpool of the despair of Charybdis. Only, like Ulysses, for all his adventurousness, he was always trying to get home. To vary the metaphor, his face was for ever turning like the sunflower towards the sun, even if it were behind a cloud; and perhaps after all there is nothing truer than the too familiar phrase from the diary of the doctor or the nurse; that he was a sick child, who passed his life in trying to get well.

CHAPTER VI

THE STYLE OF STEVENSON

THE STYLE OF STEVENSON

BEFORE writing this chapter I ought to explain that I am quite incapable of writing it; at least as many serious literary authorities think it ought to be written. I am one of those humble characters for whom the main matter of style is concerned with making a statement; and generally, in the case of Stevenson, with telling a story. Style takes its own most living and therefore most fitting form from within; as the narrative quickens and leaps, or the statement becomes warm or weighty, by being either authoritative or argumentative. The sentence takes its shape from motion; as it takes its motion from motive. And the motive (for us outcasts) is what the man has to say. But there is a technical treatment of style for which I have a profound respect, but it is a respect for the unknown, not to say the unintelligible. I will not say it is Greek to me, for I know the Greek alphabet and I do not know the alphabet of these grammars of cadence and sequence; I can still even read the Greek Testament, but the gospel of pure and abstract English brings me no news. I salute it from afar as I do musical harmony or the higher mathematics; but I shall not introduce into this book a chapter on any of these three topics. When I speak of the style of Stevenson I mean the manner in which he could express himself in plain English, even if it were in some ways peculiar English; and I have nothing but the most elementary English with which to criticise it. I cannot use the terms of any science of language, or even any science of literature.

Mr. Max Beerbohm, whose fine and classic criticism is full of those shining depths that many mistake for shallowness, has remarked truly enough on the rather wearisome repetitions in the newspapers, which did great harm to the Stevensonian fame at the time of the Stevensonian fashion. He noticed especially that a certain phrase used by Stevenson about his early experiments in writing, that he has "played the sedulous ape" to Hazlitt or to Lamb, must be permanently kept in type in the journalistic offices, so frequently do the journalists quote it. There are about a thousand things in Stevenson much more worth quoting, and much more really enlightening about his education in letters. Every young writer, however original, does begin by imitating other people, consciously or unconsciously, and nearly every old writer would be quite as willing to admit it. The real irony in the incident seems never to have been noticed. The real reason why this confession of plagiarism, out of a hundred such confessions, is always quoted, is because the confession itself has the stamp not of plagiarism but of personal originality. In the very act of claiming to have copied other styles, Stevenson writes most unmistakably in his own style. I think I could have guessed amid a hundred authors who had used the expression "played the sedulous ape." I do not think that Hazlitt would have added that word "sedulous." Some might say he was the better because the simpler without it; some would say that the word is in the strict sense too *recherché;* some might say it can be recognised because it is strained or affected. All that is matter for argument; but it is rather a joke when so individual a trick is made a proof of being merely imitative. Anyhow, that sort of trick, the rather curious combination of two such words, is the thing I mean by the style of Stevenson.

In the case of Stevenson, criticism has always tended to be hypercriticism. It is as if the critic were strung up to be as strict with the artist as the artist was with himself. But they are not very consistent or considerate in the matter. They blame him for being fastidious; and so become more fastidious themselves. They condemn him for wasting time in trying to find the right word; and then waste more time in not very successful attempts to prove it is the wrong word. I remember that Mr. George Moore (who at least led the attack when Stevenson was alive and at the height of his popularity) professed in a somewhat mysterious manner to have exposed or exploded the whole trick of Stevenson, by dwelling at length on the word "interjected": in the passage which describes a man stopping a clock with interjected finger. There seemed to be some notion that because the word is unusual in that use, it showed that there was nothing but artificial verbalism in the whole tragedy of *Jekyll and Hyde* or the fun of *The Wrong Box*. I think it is time that this sort of fastidiousness about fastidiousness should be corrected with a little common sense. The obvious question to ask Mr. Moore, if he objects to the word "interjected," is, "What word would you use?" He would immediately discover that any other word would be much weaker and even much less exact. To say "interposed finger" would suggest by its very sound a much clumsier and less precise action; "interjected" suggests by its very sound a sort of jerk of neatness; a mechanical neatness correcting mechanism. In other words, it suggests what it was meant to suggest. Stevenson used the word because it was the right word. Nobody else used it, because nobody else thought of it. And that is the whole story of Stevensonian style.

Literature is but language; it is only a rare and amazing miracle by which a man really says what he means. It is inevitable that most conversation should be convention; as when we cover a myriad beautiful contrasts or comedies of opposites by calling any number of different people "nice." Some writers, including Stevenson, desired (in the old and proper sense) to be more nice in their discrimination of niceness. Now whether we like such fastidious felicities or no, whether we are individually soothed or irritated by a style like that of Stevenson, whether we have any personal or impersonal reason for impatience with the style or the man, we ought really to have enough critical impartiality and justice to see what is the literary test. The test is whether the words are well or ill chosen, not for the purpose of fitting our own taste in words, but for the purpose of satisfying everybody's sense of the realities of things. Now it is nonsense for anybody who pretends to like literature not to see the excellence of Stevenson's expression in this way. He does pick the words that make the picture that he particularly wants to make. They do fix a particular thing, and not some general thing of the same sort; yet the thing is often one very difficult to distinguish from other things of the same sort. That is the craft of letters; and the craftsman made a vast multitude of such images in all sorts of materials. In this matter we may say of Stevenson very much what he said of Burns. He remarked that Burns surprised the polite world, with its æsthetes and antiquarians, by never writing poems on waterfalls, ruined castles or other recognised places of interest; the very fact, of course, which showed Burns to be a poet and not a tourist. It is always the prosaic person who demands poetic subjects. They are the only subjects about which he can possibly be poetic. But Burns, as Stevenson said, had a natural gift of lively and flexible comment that could play as easily upon one thing as another; a kirk or a tavern or a group going to market or a pair of dogs in the street. This gift must be judged by its aptness, its vividness and its range; and anybody who suggests that Stevenson's talent was only one piece of thin silver polished perpetually in its napkin does not, in the most exact and emphatic sense, know what he is talking about. Stevenson had exactly the talent he attributes to Burns of touching